Camp FJHS

The Parable of a Mission Trip

———

Cindy Mosley

Dedication

To my family for your unfailing support and encouragement.

To my friends who keep challenging me to step out on faith and touch the world with my many talents.

To the more than 2,000 students and their parents who inspire me to keep moving forward.

To Mrs. Roslyn Sprouse, my 9th grade English teacher, who taught me how to develop my thoughts into stories and essays that were readable works of art (my description).

To Maegan D., the young lady who inspired me to spend my summer doing exactly what I wanted to do: write this book!

Thank you all and may the Lord bless and keep you.

Table of Contents

INTRODUCTION

I sat at my desk on the last day of school, watching my 8th period students say goodbye to each other. Some were signing yearbooks, and others were exchanging cell numbers or leftover cupcakes and cookies from last-day-of-school parties. I scanned the room, smiling, as I contemplated the academic and social growth of this group of fourteen students. Academically, this was the perfect class. All of these students enthusiastically participated in creative lessons designed to help them develop strong algebraic thinking. Socially, this was a diverse group of individuals. Many of them professed to be Christians and they all got along really well. I take that back. Kane and Geni had a hate-love-hate relationship. Today, they appeared to be dialed in to the hate meter.

They were not a dating couple. You could almost say they were spiritual enemies. Kane and Geni disagreed about her faith and determination to share it with everyone. As I watched their exchanges and waited for the bell to ring, announcing the end of another year of school, I discovered Geni sitting alone, looking very discouraged. I wondered how much of Geni's sullen mood had to do with being sad about her last day of junior high or how much it was related to her disappointment at how the year ended. Geni looked defeated. I began to catalogue the number of students from previous years who sported that same look and realized that my students who started strongest with sharing their faith were the ones who finished with the weary look of defeat that Geni had.

I work at a public school in a small community in East Texas. A majority of my students attend church, participate in youth groups, and attend discipleship retreats. I noticed that several churches offer summer mission trips, while others sponsor retreats at the beginning of the second semester. It always amazes me to see the number of students who introduce themselves as Christians. They are so enthusiastic about their faith. They have interesting stories to tell about their summer. They are perky, positive, and practically percolating with energy.

As the first semester is well under way, they begin a transformation that is similar to the seasonal changes of a deciduous tree. They start school green, joyously waving their banners of love, and by December, the leaves begin to fade and fall off. Fortunately, they aren't dead, but many of them look drained of all life and in desperate need of something to bring back their joy.

As I reflect on Geni and Kane, I realize that junior high students who profess to be Christians face an extra set of issues that they are often not prepared to address. I developed Camp Fishermen Junior High School, or Camp FJHS, from a mini essay into this book of parables and epistles that address a few obstacles I've watched students encounter. Camp FJHS is my vision of the ideal summer camp experience. The ministry and characters are fictitious, but learning to handle opposition and rejection, knowing how to influence without being influenced, leading others to help, overcoming feelings of betrayal, and knowing how to show God's love are real issues that young Christians face at school and in their neighborhoods.

Prologue: FROM CAMP TO LIFE

Pastors Tim and Kelli waved at the last three church buses as they transported groups of junior high students home from Camp Fishermen Junior High, or Camp FJHS, a summer discipleship training camp. Camp FJHS, a vision of the co-pastors' youth ministry, was designed to train and prepare young Christians to maintain momentum when returning to life away from camp and church.

FJHS was a week-long camp filled with activities that reflect Christ's ministry. Each day began with prayer and praise led by Pastors Tim and Kelli, along with a band of college-age musicians who spent one summer semester serving as disciple training interns. Prayer and praise were followed by breakfast and community service projects.

The entire camp divided into groups of fourteen to mow yards and make household repairs for the elderly, serve food to children who frequented the "every child eats" program, and box food for *Meals on Wheels*. Groups of twelve students led by two adult interns served in various local communities in the mornings. During community service time, students invited community members to the camp for a Friendship Festival that offered a live band, carnival booths, and other activities that provided opportunities for camp participants to witness to others and share God's love in a fun atmosphere. After lunch, groups returned to the camp site for swimming, fishing, boating, and relaxing before the evening meal. After evening meals, the student groups met again for Bible study before going to bed.

During the closing day service, Pastors Tim and Kelli encouraged students to recall what they learned about Christ when they return home. Participants were also encouraged to send updates about their experiences and to ask for help when needed. The service was closed with a prayer and a promise of visits from the pastors and group leaders during the school year.

Following camp, in October, Pastors Tim and Kelli and group leaders began visiting schools. After each visit, the adults would meet to discuss what they learned and address issues students were facing. They collaborated on how to respond to students who were checking in through emails and letters. They decided to create a blog featuring the emails and letters along with their responses.

FACING OPPOSITION AND REJECTION

> *"No one can come to me unless the Father who sent me draws him."*
>
> -- Jesus

From: Jayd Williams

Date: October 18

To: FJHS Ministries

Hi Pastors Tim & Kelli,

First of all, I am so glad you gave us your email address. I'm glad you visited our school today, too. When you asked me if everything was going well, I didn't tell you everything.

School started off nice. I made new friends and connected with other people from our church group. There is one guy from our church who drives me CRAZY! The first week of school, Ty asked why do I believe in God and why am I always carrying my Bible. He even had the nerve to ask me how I know God cares. I got so mad and it seems like every day he pokes fun at me about being a Christian. In one of my classes, I have a couple of Christian friends who help me defend my point of view, but we all end up yelling at each other in the middle of a math lesson.

Our teacher gets frustrated and I think she picks on me because I am a Christian. She always addresses me when the yelling starts, but Ty is the one who starts it. One day she asked us Christian kids, "Why would he want to serve your God when you're always yelling at him?" I couldn't believe she said that. She finally told us that her "mercy meter" was broken and any more outbursts would result in disciplinary action for all involved. It's not fair that Ty gets to aggravate us like that and then we get in trouble. Last week, I asked to speak to Mrs. Greves about it after class. She listened to my thoughts, smiled, and said, "Instead of trying to convince Ty with your words, try showing him by your actions. Christ didn't defend His ministry. He lived it and others followed."

It's Sunday night and I am getting ready for the week. I am praying about how to act in front of Ty now. Maybe Mrs. Greves is right. I do need to be different. Thank you again for being there for us. Have a good week.

Your friend in Christ,
Your friend for life,

Jayd

From: FJHS Ministries

Date: October 18

Reply to Jayd Williams

Hey Jayd,

It sounds like your school year has a great start. We know you may not feel that way, but trust us, you're in a good place right now.

We're sending you a list of Scriptures that might encourage you as you make your way through this journey at school. Your teacher is right, by the way. We love you and will continue to pray that the Spirit of the Lord rests upon you, and that you will have the Spirit of wisdom and understanding, the Spirit of counsel and might, the Spirit of knowledge, and the fear of the Lord. And that your delight shall be in the fear of the Lord (Isaiah 11:2, 3).

Proverbs 15:1

Galatians 6:9

2 Thessalonians 3:3

Proverbs 3:5, 6

Keep in touch.

P T & K, FJHS ministries

Reflection:

Jayd appears to be frustrated with her situation at school and feels that she needs to defend her choice to believe.

Can you think of a time when you felt the need to defend your choice to believe?

_____

_____

_____

_____

_____

Do you know of other Scriptures that might be helpful when others don't understand you?

_____

_____

_____

_____

_____

Prayer:

Father in Heaven, please teach me how to live before others so they will want to know You. Amen.

BETRAYED BY A BELIEVER

> *"I neither know nor understand what you mean."*
>
> -- Peter

From: Martin Cambry

Date: October 26

To: FJHS Ministries

Dear Pastors Tim & Kelli,

FCA was really good today. I'm glad you were the guest speakers. I really needed to hear what you said today about Peter's dilemma. I guess you can call me "Peter" because I don't think—no, I know I have denied Christ by my actions.

I did what you said by connecting to a local church after camp. I made friends with kids in the youth group. I even made friends with a guy on the football team who goes to my church. Until a few weeks ago, I thought he was my friend. We were in the locker room and some of the guys were saying some pretty nasty stuff about a girl. I told them that they were being disrespectful and should stop. They basically told me to shut the F up and stop being a wuss. I got so mad that I walked away.

Later on in the week, we were on the bus coming home from a game and the same guys were asking people if they had finished their homework. They wanted to copy. I had just finished mine, but I didn't say anything. My "friend" Josh told them I had mine. I refused to give them my paper and put it in my duffle bag. As we unloaded the bus, Josh shoved me down in the seat while the other guys jumped on me and took my duffle bag. They threw all of my stuff on the floor. One of them took my homework.

I am so mad. I haven't been to church in two weeks now. Yesterday a teacher who goes to my church told me she missed seeing me at church. She also told me that she can see a difference in how I act at school. She said that some of my other teachers have talked about how angry and disrespectful I've become. All I did was look at her. I didn't have anything to say.

I can't believe Josh turned on me like that. He claims he is a Christian. I don't hang out with anyone anymore. I'm still in athletics and I act like everything is alright, but I can't wait until basketball season is over so I don't have to act like a team player. If I go talk to the coach, I will be a snitch. If I go to Pastor Rusty, he will probably bring me and Josh in together and I'm just not ready for that. Josh is a fake and I don't want him going back to his buddies at school telling them about me.

What am I supposed to do? My dad works out of town a lot and is gone all the time. My mom is busy running my sisters and me around. She is tired and I just don't want to bother her.

I'm going to pray tonight. I haven't in a long time. I'm glad you came to the school. I know that I am forgiven and that Jesus loves me. But I'm still mad.

Pray for me.

Martin

From: FJHS Ministries
Date: October 26
Reply to Martin Cambry

Wow, Martin! You're having a rough time. We're glad you contacted us. We were very happy to see you at FCA. We're sorry you feel betrayed by Josh. We wouldn't call you "Peter," though. Do you remember what Christ did for those who betrayed Him? He prayed for them and forgave them. Being a Christian is not easy, Martin. Sometimes people love us and sometimes they hate us. Jesus told us to be glad when we experience rejection because that means we really are doing the Lord's work. When we set out to build the Kingdom of God, we will face opposition. That opposition will come in many different forms. It's like playing sports. We can be on a good team, but we still have to work hard and practice. If we want to win, we have to have a game plan. In football, there is a play book. As Christians, our Bible is our play book.

We are praying for you that God will heal your heart and give you wisdom to know how to walk and be a light where there appears to be darkness. Be brave and keep praying. Remember, forgiveness is essential in this walk.

You know Pastor Rusty is right, don't you? You need to talk to Josh. Christians seek peace and you need to make peace with Josh. We're sending you some Scriptures that we think might encourage you.

I Samuel 17 (David faces his brothers and the giant)
Galatians 6:9
Genesis 37 - 44 (Joseph's life)

Hey, Martin, there is a purpose for your distress. Hang in there.

We love you.
Keep in touch.

PT&K, FJHS Ministries

Reflection:

Josh is angry and feels betrayed by his friend and teammates.

Why does Josh feel like he is denying Christ by his actions?

_____

_____

_____

_____

What do you think Josh should do?

_____

_____

_____

_____

Can you find examples of other betrayals in the Bible? List them here.

_____

_____

_____

_____

Prayer: Holy Father, give us courage to speak the truth in love, seek to be at peace with others, and to forgive when people we care about disappoint us. Amen.

LOVING THE LOST

> *"If God so loved us, we also ought to love one another."*
>
> -- John

From: Zayla Rose Torrey

Date: November 4

To: FJHS Ministries

Hi Pastors T & Kelli,

I was so excited to see you on our campus today! I'm having a great year at school! I was really nervous about starting junior high this year, especially after what happened this summer.

After FJHS camp, I spent two weeks with my grandma. I love going to Big Mama's house when no one else is there. I get SPOILED! I go spend the second week in August with her every year so I can go to the annual revival at her church. This year was extra special because I understood what the preacher was talking about!

Every night I got to learn more about being a Christian and during the day I hung out with friends in the neighborhood. I tried to get my two best friends to go to church with us for "bring a friend night."

Arri and Paul couldn't believe I wanted to go to church instead of going skating. They even laughed when I told them I spend time reading my Bible every day. They hurt my feelings. I'm OK, though. I have made some new friends, and I pray for Arri and Paul. I really hope they come to know Christ as their Savior.

I'm so glad I went to camp! I used to watch church on TV on the Sundays when we didn't go. I would see churches talk about mission trips and wondered what it would be like to go. FJHS felt like what I think a mission trip should be like. Honestly, going to junior high is like a mission trip, too. I never thought about how many people don't go to church or are not Christians until this year. I find myself praying a lot for people I don't know. The halls and classes are filled with mean and disrespectful people. I don't talk to them all, but I do pray for them. I'm so glad I learned how to pray for others at FJHS.

I hope to see you soon!

Zayla

From: FJHS Ministries

Date: November 4

Reply to Zayla Rose Torrey

Hey Zayla Rose!

Wow! You sound like you are having a great time in junior high. We love your approach to getting along at school. We know some grownups who struggle with getting along in life. You have figured out how to help people without getting caught up in their mess or bad choices.

We admire your determination to pray for others. We like to pray Scriptures over others and so we are sending you some Scriptures that we think will help you intercede for people at your school.

Ephesians 1:16 - 20

I Thessalonians 5:23

Jeremiah 17:14 (You can put names of the people in place of the words "you" or "me.")

Keep up the good work! We love you, Zayla Rose!

P T & K, FJHS Ministries

Reflection:

Zayla is determined to show love to others. She not only shows kindness to nice people, but also to those who struggle to do what is right.

What other ways can Zayla show love on her campus?

_____

_____

_____

_____

What would you do if two of your friends laughed at you about your faith in God?

_____

_____

_____

_____

Can you find more Scriptures about loving others?

_____

_____

_____

_____

Prayer:

Heavenly Father, show me how to love others in a way that reflects Your love for us. Amen

> *"We will not serve your gods or worship your golden image."*
> -- Shadrach, Meshach, and Abednego

From: Josh Freeman

Date: November 11

To: FJHS Ministries

Today was awesome! You rocked FCA this morning. I don't know if you talked to Martin or not, but we don't hang out anymore. He kept acting like he was so much better than everybody else, always telling people what to do and how to act.

I made friends with some guys in athletics. I knew they weren't Christians, so I started hanging out with them to try to get to know them and invite them to church. They came a few times and so we hang out now. The only problem, besides getting into it with Martin, is we get in trouble a lot. We really don't do anything, except laugh and talk a lot. One of my teachers called my parents and told then I have changed and that I'm hanging out with a bad group of kids. We don't do anything wrong. Well, one time we needed help with our homework and asked Martin to help us. He told us no, so we borrowed his to finish ours. That wasn't my idea, but I didn't do anything to stop it. That's probably why Martin doesn't hang out with me anymore and my teachers don't seem to like me anymore, either. Some other kids won't have anything to do with us because they say we cheat. We aren't really cheating; we just need help sometimes.

My parents are talking about changing my school because of the negative reports. I'm just trying to get more people to come to church. Should I stop hanging out with my new friends? They're not that bad. They just like to have fun and area a little loud sometimes. They aren't Christians yet, but that's why I'm supposed to bring them to church, right?

Josh

From: FJHS Ministries
Date: November 11
Reply to Josh Freeman

Hey Josh,

It sounds like you've some interesting things going on. We're glad you got in touch with us. It was good to see you at FCA. We're sorry to hear that you and Martin are having problems. Do you think you've gotten in over your head with your new friends?

We know sometimes it is not easy being more of an influence than being influenced by others. There is a Scripture that says, "Do not conform to the world (things that are not godlike) but be transformed by changing your mind" (Romans 12:2). You have to stay true to Christ, no matter who you're with or where you go. It's great that you are inviting your friends to church, but make sure you introduce them to others, especially the youth pastor. Help your friends become friends with people who help you be a stronger Christian. We will pray for you and your new friends.

We are sending you a few Scriptures that might help you make decisions about your friendships.

Numbers 13 & 14 (Joshua and Caleb having to stand for what they believe when others disagree.)
Ephesians 6:10 - 18 (Arming yourself for your daily walk)

By the way, we think it might be a good idea to talk to Pastor Rusty about what happened with you and Martin.

Keep in touch.
PT & K, FJHS Ministries

Reflection:

Josh is struggling with making good choices.

What are some choices he is making that do not reflect Christ?

_____

_____

_____

_____

What are some things Josh could do to fix his relationship with Martin and keep his new friends?

_____

_____

_____

_____

What are some Scriptures Josh could use to help him remember his role in leading others to Christ?

_____

_____

_____

_____

Prayer:

Heavenly Father, teach us how to be a light for you when others seem to want to walk in darkness. Amen.

ENCOURAGING YOURSELF

> *"I strengthened myself in the Lord."*
>
> -- David

From: Krystal Stone

Date: December 3

To: FJHS Ministries

Hey PT&K!

Thanks for coming to group today. I love it that my school has a support group that helps us get a fresh start after being in trouble. When my parents moved me to this charter school, I was glad. I just couldn't stand being around all those fake people at my old school. At this school, everybody just wants to get their credits so they can graduate and there's not much time for messy stuff.

The group sessions are so helpful! I used to be so depressed. It was hard trying to stop smoking, especially when my parents were always having parties and trying to get me to get high with them and their friends. You know I kept getting in trouble for being absent from school before I moved here.

Now, since I've been going to Group and church, I'm doing so much better. I haven't cut myself or gotten high for three months now. Not only do I feel better, but my grades are also better.

Do you like my new hair color? I do! I like feeling normal! I know baby blue may not seem normal to some people, but it is so much better than ink black. I'm glad God made me special and that I am truly loved by Him. My parents may not sacrifice for me, but Jesus did!

I've made friends with this really nice girl named Rubie. We have so much in common. It turns out that she was depressed, too, because her mom abused her when she was little. The lady who comes to lead our support group, Ms. Kay, is really cool. She also leads group at Rubie's school. Rubie used to talk about killing herself a lot, but Ms. Kay became her friend. She introduced us because she thought we could help each other be strong. It's nice having someone to talk to who understands what you're going through. Rubie and I get together every weekend and we video chat almost every day.

When my parents throw wild parties, I lock myself in my room or stay with Rubie at her grandma's house. She takes us to church. Their church is a little different than what I expected. I thought the minister was going to yell at us and tell us all the things we needed to change. He doesn't do that. He reminds us of God's love for us and shows us in the Bible how we are supposed to treat ourselves and others.

Rubie and I have learned how to love ourselves. We've learned how to forgive our parents and we are both less depressed. I'm going to bring Rubie to FJHS with me next summer. You are going to love her. Please keep praying for us and help us pray for our parents. We want them to stop drinking and doing drugs. We want them to become Christians.

Thanks again. I love you both.

Krystal

From: FJHS Ministries
Date: December 3
Reply to Krystal Stone

Hey Krystal!

Maybe you and Rubie could video chat with us sometimes. We would love to meet Rubie. It sounds like you are taking care of yourself spiritually and emotionally. Ms. Kay is a blessing and your schools are showing that they really care about bringing her in to help you guys.

We will help you pray for your parents. When we pray, we like to use Scriptures to guide your prayers. We are sending you the Scriptures that we will use to pray for your family and you can pray them, as well.

Jeremiah 17:14 and 29:11 - 13
Malachi 4:5 (Praying that the Lord will turn the hearts of your parents back to you.)

So glad to hear from you and that you are doing so well. We love you! Baby blue hair looks good on you and so does that smile you were sporting the last time we saw you.

P T & K, FJHS Ministries

Reflection:

Krystal faced several struggles, but was able to find ways to overcome those difficulties.

What were some of Krystal's struggles?

_____

_____

_____

_____

How is Krystal able to find peace in her situation?

_____

_____

_____

_____

List some other Scriptures that Krystal might use to stay positive in her situation.

_____

_____

_____

_____

Prayer:

Lord God, You said that we would face troubles in this world. Please help us remember that You have overcome the world and that You are our refuge. Amen.

LEADING OTHERS TO HELP

> *"God is a refuge for us."*
>   -- David

From: Trey Jones

Date: December 10

To: FJHS Ministries

Dear Pastors Tim & Kelli

You don't know me, but you were at my school today. I saw you in the hall surrounded by kids who seem to know you. I asked Martin who you were and he told me you were the leaders at the camp he went to in the summer. He also told me that you are people I could talk to and trust not to spread my business around. I need someone to trust like that.

See, my dad killed himself a couple of months ago and I am having a hard time. I live with my grandparents because I don't know my mom. She left when I was two and I haven't seen her since. Not many people at school know about my dad, but I think my teachers know because they don't yell at me anymore when I fall asleep in class. They wake me up, but they don't yell at me or send me to the office.

One of my teachers kept me after class one day and told me she thinks I'm depressed. Mrs. Greves is cool and she is a Christian. She is always playing what she calls her "Jesus music." Anyway, she told me that I should probably talk to someone, preferably an adult I can trust. So I'm contacting you.

I'm not a Christian. I don't even know what that is, but Martin said being a Christian could make all the difference in my life. I need something different in my life. My grandparents told me my dad's depression led to his suicide. I feel depressed. Does that mean I'm going to commit suicide? I heard a kid in my class say that people who commit suicide go to Hell. What does that mean? I just want a normal life. I don't feel like doing anything but sleep. I know I should be grateful I have my grandparents, but they act like they are scared to talk to me.

Can you help me?

Trey

From: FJHS Ministries
Date: December 10
Reply to Trey Jones

Hello Trey,
We are so glad you contacted us. We're sorry to hear about your dad. We understand you must be going through a tough time and having

someone to turn to during tough times is very important to help you feel better. Martin has a good point. Being a Christian can be helpful during hard times. Being a Christian means that you have decided to accept Jesus as Lord of your life and you are choosing to live by His example. We would love to meet you and share more.

Just because you are depressed doesn't mean you are going to commit suicide. It means that you're sad and are having a hard time adjusting to the things going on in your life. We think you should tell your grandparents how you feel and maybe ask them to find a counselor for you to talk to. You also have a school counselor who can help you.

We are planning to be at Martin's youth group on Wednesday. Why don't you come? We would love to meet you. You might even like what you see at the service. Until we meet, we will be praying for you to find some peace in your situation and for God to heal your broken heart.

Do you own a Bible? Reading the Bible is very helpful when you are having a hard time.

Hope to see you Wednesday.

Love and hugs,
PT&K, FJHS Ministries.

From: Trey Jones

Date: December 27

Reply to FJHS Ministries

Hey Pastors,

It was nice meeting you at church on Wednesday. Thank you for the Bible and for praying for me. I read the Scriptures you gave me. They help a lot.

I talked to the school counsellor and she told me that I am not the only student who had a parent to die in the last year. She has a support group here on campus for those of us who have dead parents. I'm glad you told me to talk to her. We all had lunch together yesterday and we meet every week. She told us it is an open door group. We can choose to come or not. She said that after a while, some of us may not feel like we need to meet. I am feeling better, but I'm going to keep going for a while.

I don't sleep in class as much and I have made some friends. Martin is really cool. I'm not in athletics, but he still sits at my table at lunch and chose me to be his study partner in math class today. For the first time in a long time, I feel like everything is going to be all right.

Thank you again.

Trey

Reflection:

Trey was depressed and needed help. Martin was wise to refer him to adults. There are times when it is best to lead others to help rather than try ourselves.

What are ways Martin showed Trey the love of God?

_____

_____

_____

_____

Some people said some scary things to Trey about his situation. What are some encouraging words you could say without causing more pain?

_____

_____

_____

_____

List some Scriptures that might help encourage someone who is depressed.

_____

_____

_____

_____

Prayer:

Father in Heaven, give me words to speak that will bless and encourage others. Amen.

PROTECTING THE HEART

> *"Whoever guards his mouth preserves his life."*
>
> -- King Solomon

FJHS Ministries Blog's Friday Night Chat

PT&K:

Hey Kiddos,

We thought we could have a live chat tonight. Our topic is, "Does it matter what movies we watch or what music we listen to?" Join in the discussion when you want and sign off when you need to go.

Sara:

I don't think it matters as long as we pray, read our Bibles, and go to church.

Kris:

I don't know about that. Some of the words in some music are crude. I don't want to hear them. And some movies, even the ones on TV, have bad words.

Sara:

Then don't listen. Pick something else that you like. Not all music and movies have bad words.

Thalya:

The music I like does have bad words. My parents will only let me listen to clean versions and they only let me watch G- or PG-rated movies they have watched first. They even do random ear bud checks to make sure I am not listening to something with bad words.

PT & K:

Did they tell you why, Thalya?

Thalya:

Yes. They said even though I am a Christian, it matters what I listen to. I may not practice using bad words, but if I listen to them a lot, I might slip up and use one. They even had me do an experiment one day to prove their point.

Staci:

What kind of experiment?

Thalya:

They gave me two zip-up plastic bags and two paper towels. I folded the paper towels and wet them before putting in the bags. They put a spoon full of crushed moth balls in one bag and some drops of fabric softener in the other. I sealed both bags and let them sit for a week. We wrote "bad words" on the moth ball bag and "good words" on the fabric softener bag. When we took them out, I could smell both bags. They told me my heart and mind are like the paper towels. I absorb what I see and hear. After a while, it becomes evident, either by my words or actions.

Sara:

I never thought of it that way.

PT&K:

I like that experiment. You know that experiment is like a living parable. Kudos to your parents, Thalya. Does anyone know of any Scriptures that might relate to this topic?

Thalya:

My parents had me memorize Matthew 15:18 (AMP)" "But whatever [word] comes out of the mouth comes from the heart, and this is what defiles *ana* dishonors the man."

PT&K:

That is a good one, Thalya. Here is a challenge for you all. See if you can find other Scriptures that might apply and post them.

Josh:

Ephesians 4:29 (CEV): "Stop all your dirty talk. Say the right thing at the right time and help others by what you say."

PT&K:

Hey Josh! Glad you could join us. Good word, Bro!

Sara:

Isaiah 55:7 (ESV): "Let the wicked forsake his way, and the unrighteous man his thoughts; let him return to the LORD, that he may have compassion on him, and to our God, for he will abundantly pardon."

PT&K:

Thanks, Sara! Aren't you glad God forgives us when we turn to Him?

Staci:

Proverbs 15:26 (TLB): "The Lord hates the thoughts of the wicked but delights in kind words."

PT&K:

Staci that is one of our favorites. It reminds us that the Lord knows what we are thinking, even if we don't say what is on our mind.

Krystal:

I love a challenge! James 3:5-6 (The Message): "It only takes a spark, remember, to set off a forest fire. A careless or wrongly placed word out of your mouth can do that. By our speech we can ruin the world, turn harmony to chaos, throw mud on a reputation, send the whole world up in smoke and go up in smoke with it, smoke right from the pit of hell."

PT&K:

Good one, Krystal! That Scripture is a challenge for us to be very careful about what we say.

Kris:

I haven't found a Scripture yet. I'm going to add these to my memory verses.

PT&K:

It's OK that you haven't found one, Kris. You have a good strategy there. The more good that you take in, the more good that will come out.

This was a great chat, ladies and gentlemen.

Let's meet again next week.

Grace and peace be to you all.

Reflection:

Does it matter what music you listen to, what movies you watch, or what books you read?

_____

_____

_____

_____

Thalya's parents used an experiment to demonstrate the importance of guarding your heart. The experiment gave insight and wisdom. The book of Proverbs refers to wisdom and insight together numerous times. Having wisdom and insight can help you make good choices.

List some Proverbs that refer to the importance of having wisdom and insight.

_____

_____

_____

_____

_____

Prayer:

Lord, let my thoughts and actions be acceptable to you. Lead me on a path that brings glory to Your name. Amen.

> *"Whoever believes in the Son has*
> *eternal life."*
>
>   -- John

From: Chase Rivers

Date: January 9

To: FJHS Ministries

Dear Pastors,

You don't know me, but I got your email address from a flyer being passed out by some dudes at lunch last week. I didn't think I would, but I keep running into this girl named Zayla in the hall. She is always smiling and being nice to people. She is even nice to me.

I am probably the worst student in the school. I get into fights a lot and I have the hook-up for those who want cigarettes or weed. I have been to ISS so many times, I can't count and I just got back from an alternative school. I got caught with tobacco on campus.

Zayla isn't the only person who is nice to me. I have this teacher who told me she was really glad I was back in class. I told her I didn't believe her. She asked me why. I told her that I have never had a teacher who liked me or cared about me. She told me she loves me and she knew that I could make good choices. She told me I have potential. No one has ever said something like that about me.

That Zayla girl invited me to church and I laughed at her. She told me I would like the group leaders at her church. Those are the guys passing out flyers. They come to lunch every Wednesday. Zayla introduced them to me, but I really didn't have anything to say to them. They told me God loves me and has a plan for my life. Can God really love somebody like me? I mess up all the time. My parents don't even love me. They call me a screw up and tell me all the time that I am never going to amount to anything. I want to prove them wrong. What can I do? Is there hope for me? Sometimes I wish I was never born.

Chase

From: FJHS Ministries
Date: January 9
Reply to Chase Rivers

Hey Chase,

Pastors Jeremiah and Eli told us they met you. We've been praying that you would contact us. Yes, God loves you, man. Zayla and your teachers are people God has placed in your life to show you unconditional love. That's the kind of love He has for you. It doesn't matter how bad you think you are. He has this thing called grace that is like a never-ending fountain of love.

You see, God made us all and He knew that we would make mistakes. He made a way for us to be forgiven for our mistakes and to experience His love. Jesus paid the price for all of our sins—past and future—on the cross. He gave His life so that we could live. In order to receive that forgiveness, we must believe that Jesus died on the cross for our sins and rose again to live with God in Heaven. The Bible teaches us that if we confess with our mouth that we believe Jesus is our Savior and died for our sins, then we are saved.

Pastors Jeremiah and Eli will return to your campus next week. They have a gift for you. We hope you feel confident enough to talk to them. We will be on your campus next month and hope to meet you then. You can contact us any time you have questions or need someone to talk to.

Love and prayers.

PT&K, FJHS Ministries

From: Chase Rivers

Date: January 31

Reply to FJHS Ministries

Dear Pastors,

I'm a Christian!

I sat with Pastors Jeremiah and Eli at lunch a couple of weeks ago. They invited me to youth group that night and I went. I learned so much about God's love and forgiveness. We prayed what they called the believer's prayer and now I'm saved. I have a Bible now and another book they said would help me understand what it means to be born again. Going to church is a new experience for me.

I haven't been in trouble at school in two weeks. I used to get in trouble almost every day. My parents keep looking at me and asking what kind of trouble I'm getting into. I told them I've changed, but they don't believe me. I don't care. I like knowing I am loved by somebody. I like having someone believe in me. I want to believe in myself. I'm going to make better grades and stay out of my usual trouble. I want a new beginning and it looks like I have one.

Chase

From: FJHS Ministries

Date: January 31

Reply to Chase Rivers

Chase, we are so happy!

We are rejoicing that you have a new life ahead of you. We believe in you. It is important for you to stay connected to a local church and surround yourself with people to care about your spiritual growth.

We will see you next week when we come to your campus. Have a great week and keep in touch.

We are so happy. May the Lord God who created you set you apart for His service and keep you. May He bless you with peace and courage to do all that He created you to accomplish?

P T & K, FJHS Ministries

Reflection:

Chase was introduced to Christianity by Zayla and his teacher, but they didn't overwhelm him with words.

What are some ways Zayla and Chase's teacher introduced him to Christ?

_____

_____

_____

_____

What are some ways you can introduce others to Christ?

_____

_____

_____

_____

Make a list of Scriptures you could use to help someone come to believe and become a Christian.

_____

_____

_____

_____

Prayer:

Holy Father, there are so many people who don't know You and are hurting for someone to love them. Teach me how to love them so they will come to know You. Amen.

COMING SOON!

Camp FJHS: The parable of a discipleship retreat

Camp FJHS: The parable of a mission trip concludes the first semester of ministry for Pastors Tim & Kelli and their team of interns. After reflecting over the issues addressed in the first semester, they decided that the second semester needed careful planning. Their disciples were showing growth pains and in order to finish strong, a retreat would be necessary.

The parable of a discipleship retreat will uncover more obstacles young believers are facing. The team has invited youth groups from local churches and FCA groups from local schools to participate in a weekend retreat. Instead of watching a movie the team has decided to break the retreaters into groups of actors who will act out concerns and how to overcome new set of challenges. Camp leaders soon discover that providing students an outlet for their concerns will open discussions about divorce in Christian homes, grieving the loss of a friend in a tragic accident, forgiveness, starting over after a move, harmful relationships, and intimacy with God.

ABOUT THE AUTHOR

Cindy lives with her husband, Frank, and their son Taylon in East Texas. Cindy has taught 7th and 8th grade math for 14 years and enjoys reading books, mixed media art, and writing inspiring stories. Visit Cindy's blog at cimowrites.com to view her latest creations.

www.ingramcontent.com/pod-product-compliance
Lightning Source LLC
Chambersburg PA
CBHW060627030426
42337CB00018B/3229